Fossils and Rocks

by Kimberly M. Hutmacher

Science Content Editor:
Shirley Duke

Rourke
Educational Media

rourkeeducationalmedia.com

Teacher Notes available at
rem4teachers.com

Science Content Editor: Shirley Duke holds a bachelor's degree in biology and a master's degree in education from Austin College in Sherman, Texas. She taught science in Texas at all levels for twenty-five years before starting to write for children. Her science books include *You Can't Wear These Genes, Infections, Infestations, and Diseases, Enterprise STEM, Forces and Motion at Work, Environmental Disasters,* and *Gases.* She continues writing science books and also works as a science content editor.

Photo credits: © Marcio Silva; Pages 2/3 © markrhiggins; Pages 4/5 © Turovsky, holbox, Aaron Amat, Graça Victoria, Volodymyr Krasyuk, Atiketta Sangasaeng, J. Helgason, Andrey Burmakin, EugenP, Zelenskaya; Pages 6/7 © Rob kemp, dmitriyd, Publio Furbino; Pages 8/9 © Vulkanette, Joy Prescott; Pages 10/11 © Coprid, Aleksandr Bryliaev, Tyler Boyes, schankz, Michal Baranski, maxim ibragimov, Mark Yarchoan; Pages 12/13 © markrhiggins; Pages 14/15 © Rich Koele, Dr. Morley Read; Pages 16/17 © Roy Palmer, StanOd, Caitlin Mirra; Pages 18/19 © Steve Richmond, Bill Florence; Pages 20/21 © antoni halim, ded pixto

Editor: Kelli Hicks

My Science Library series produced by Blue Door Publishing, Florida for Rourke Educational Media.

Library of Congress PCN Data

Hutmacher, Kimberly M.
 Fossils and Rocks / Kimberly M. Hutmacher.
   p. cm. -- (My Science Library)
 ISBN 978-1-61810-103-7 (Hard cover) (alk. paper)
 ISBN 978-1-61810-236-2 (Soft cover)
 Library of Congress Control Number: 2011943573

Rourke Educational Media
Printed in the United States of America,
North Mankato, Minnesota

rourkeeducationalmedia.com

customerservice@rourkeeducationalmedia.com
PO Box 643328 Vero Beach, Florida 32964

Table of Contents

You're Standing on a Rock!

Did you know that you're standing on a **rock**? Planet Earth's outer layer is a gigantic rock. Sometimes the rock is covered by soil, grass, or water, but the rock is still there.

Earth's outer layer is called the crust.

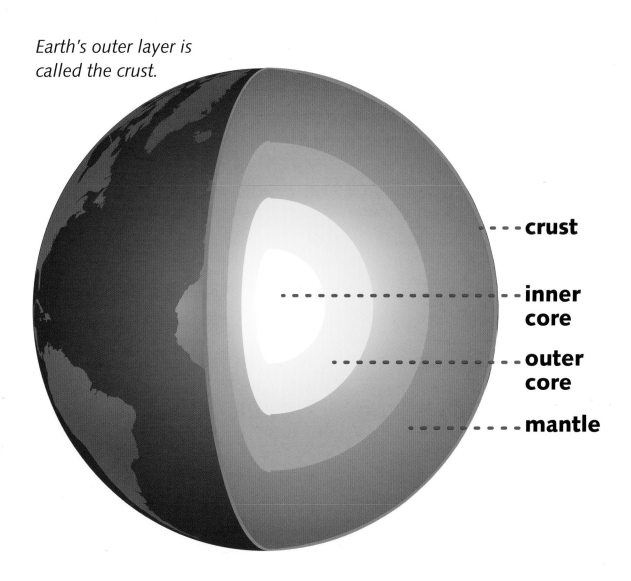

crust

inner core

outer core

mantle

Minerals are natural, non-living particles found in the ground. Minerals, tightly packed together, form rock.

There are almost 5,000 known minerals! Here are some you've probably seen.

clay	salt	talc
diamond	emerald	ruby
gold	silver	copper

Rockin' Families

●●●●●●●●●●●●●●●●●●●●●

Rock is used in everyday life. When we see cement driveways, marble floors, ceramic tiles, or granite counter tops, we are looking at the wonders of rock!

Any rock you ever find will belong to one of three different rock families: **igneous**, **sedimentary**, or **metamorphic**.

Pumice is a form of igneous rock that we use to buff away dry skin.

Quartzite is a form of metamorphic rock. It's often dyed and used to make carvings and jewelry.

This sedimentary rock formation is in Mesa Monument Valley, Arizona.

magma

Igneous rocks form from fire. Deep within Earth's crust is a hot, melted rock called **magma**. Magma squeezes slowly, like toothpaste from a tube, into cracks and crevices between the layers of rock underground. This magma cools and hardens, forming rock. Igneous rock also forms when magma is forced out of Earth from a volcanic eruption. Again, once the lava cools, it hardens into rock.

Sediment consists of mud, rock, sand, and the dead remains of once living organisms. Sediment settles in layers at the bottom of oceans, rivers, and lakes. Over time, these layers are pressed and buried. Water trickles in through tiny cracks, bringing minerals with it. Minerals work like glue, pressing the sediment together and forming sedimentary rock.

Some common forms of sedimentary rock are sandstone, limestone, and shale.

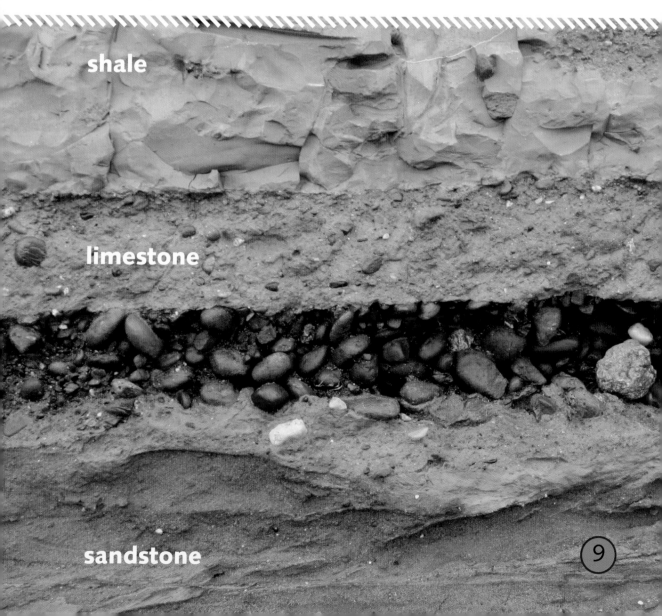

shale

limestone

sandstone

Have you ever mixed together ingredients to make a loaf of bread? Before baking, the dough is gooey and squishy.

After baking, the dough changes into a light, fluffy loaf of bread. Rock also bakes and changes. Igneous and sedimentary rock are baked by magma. When this happens, the rock is crushed. This new, changed rock forms metamorphic rock.

The Rock Cycle

●○○○○●○○○○●○○○○●○○○○●○○○○

The rock cycles happens slowly, over thousands of years. First, magma pours from volcanoes, forming new rock. While this is happening, old rock is chipped, broken, and worn away by wind and water.

This never-ending process of the breaking down of old rock and the making of new rock is called the **rock cycle**. Rock always changes!

Weathering and Erosion
Compaction and Cementation
Heat and Pressure
Cooling
Melting

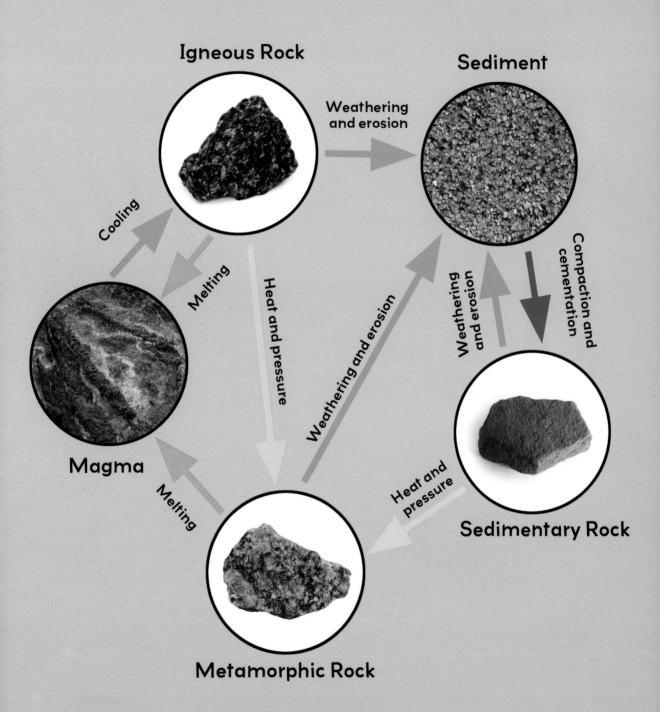

Igneous Rock

Sediment

Weathering
and erosion

Cooling

Melting

Heat and pressure

Weathering and erosion

Weathering
and erosion

Compaction and
cementation

Magma

Melting

Heat and
pressure

Sedimentary Rock

Metamorphic Rock

Planet Earth's history is told in its rocks. **Fossils** are the remains or imprints of plants and animals that lived long ago. These imprints or remains get **preserved** in Earth's crust.

Two Kinds of Fossils

Body Fossils
These are stone imprints, molds, or casts left by organisms that were once living. They include animals, plants, and people. Single teeth or bones are body fossils, too.

Trace Fossils
Footprints, tracks, eggs, and fossilized excrement are trace fossils.

A mammoth skull found at a dig site in South Dakota.

Fossils give us a peek into the lives of the people, plants, and animals that lived long ago. They tell us where they lived, how they lived, and what the world was like around them.

You can find fossils all over the world. Chances are good that no matter where in the world you live, you will find fossils underground or underfoot.

Forming Fossils

It's not easy to become a fossil. Most of the fossils that scientists find are bones or shells. Many soft animals, like worms, never become fossils. Even animals with bones and shells don't always become fossils.

Many animals rot or get eaten by other animals before they have the chance to fossilize.

This is a fossilized trilobite. Trilobites lived in shallow seas about 600 million years ago. Evidence of trilobites has been found on every continent.

After an animal dies, layers of sediments are deposited on top of earlier layers. The massive weight of the water and upper layers press down on the bones, forming an impression of their shape.

In order to fossilize, a plant or animal is buried by sediment. Over time, the sediment hardens into sedimentary rock. Most of the time, this happens under water. That's why most fossils are found in areas once covered by oceans.

Trapped animals and insects have fossilized in ice, tree sap, and tar. Mammoths were trapped and fossilized in ice.

Many mammoths were trapped and fossilized in tar pits. The La Brea tar pits in Los Angeles has the world's largest collection of ice age animal and plant fossils in the world.

Replica of a mammoth at La Brea tar pits.

Reading the Past

A **paleontologist** is a scientist who studies fossils in order to find out about life long ago. Paleontologists have discovered ways of measuring how old fossils are.

Sue

The *Tyrannosaurus rex* called Sue is an example of a large fossil that has been kept in amazing condition. Sue was discovered by Sue Hendrickson in 1990 and is on display at the Field Museum in Chicago, Illinois.

Paleontologists sometimes use a process called **radiocarbon dating** to figure out how old plants and trees are. Living plants and trees absorb carbon. A small amount of the carbon they absorb is radioactive, and it's called C_{14}. When a tree dies, C_{14} slowly leaves the tree. By measuring how much C_{14} is left, scientists can figure out when the tree died.

Fossils: Fueling Our Lives

Most of the fuels we use today to heat our homes and run our automobiles come from the remains of plants and animals that lived thousands of years ago. The remains of microscopic sea animals called **plankton** formed our oil and gas. Plants, once found in swamps, form the coal we burn today.

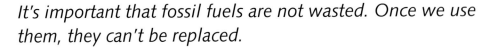

It's important that fossil fuels are not wasted. Once we use them, they can't be replaced.

We use fossil fuels when we put gas in our cars, burn natural gas to heat our homes, and burn coal to make electricity.

These plants and animals were changed by heat and pressure. The carbon in them became **fossil fuels**. Fossils not only tell the stories of our past, they contribute to our present and our future sources of fuel.

When we learn about fossils and rocks we are really studying Earth's history and the possibilities for the future.

Show What You Know

1. Name the three different groups of rock.

2. Describe two ways in which plants or animals can become fossils.

3. Name two fossil fuels. Compare and contrast where they came from.

Glossary

fossil fuels (FOSS-uhl FYOO-uhlz): fuels like oil, natural gas, and coal made from the remains of plants and animals from long ago

fossils (FOSS-uhlz): remains or prints of plants or animals that lived long ago

igneous (IG-nee-uhss): rocks formed by fire in Earth's crust

magma (MAG-muh): hot liquid from Earth's crust

metamorphic (met-uh-MOR-fik): rock that has been changed

minerals (MIN-ur-uhlz): a non-living substance formed in Earth naturally

paleontologist (pale-ee-uhn-TOL-uh-just): a scientist who studies fossils

plankton (PLANGK-tuhn): tiny plants and animals found floating in bodies of water

preserved (pri-ZURVD): kept in a certain condition

radiocarbon dating (RAY-dee-oh KAR-buhn dayt-ing): a process by which scientists measure how much radiocarbon is in a fossilized tree or plant to learn when it died

rock (rok): mineral matter formed as part of Earth's crust

rock cycle (rok SYE-kuhl): the process by which new rock is made and old rock is broken and worn away

sedimentary (sed-uh-MEN-tuh-ree): made by sediment

Index

Websites to Visit

www.kidsgeo.com/geology-for-kids/

www.beloit.edu/sepm/Fossil_Explorations/Trace_Fossils.html

www.fossils-facts-and-finds.com/index.html

About the Author

Kimberly M. Hutmacher is the author of 24 books for children. She loves to research science topics and share what she learns. She also enjoys sharing her love of writing with audiences of all ages.

Ask The Author!
www.rem4students.com